MW01490899

*GREATER
ALSO AVAILABLE IN EBOOK AND
AUDIOBOOK FORMAT.

Greater Than a Tourist Book Series Reviews from Readers

I think the series is wonderful and beneficial for tourists to get information before visiting the city.

-Seckin Zumbul, Izmir Turkey

I am a world traveler who has read many trip guides but this one really made a difference for me. I would call it a heartfelt creation of a local guide expert instead of just a guide.

-Susy, Isla Holbox, Mexico

New to the area like me, this is a must have!

-Joe, Bloomington, USA

This is a good series that gets down to it when looking for things to do at your destination without having to read a novel for just a few ideas.

-Rachel, Monterey, USA

Good information to have to plan my trip to this destination.

-Pennie Farrell, Mexico

Great ideas for a port day.

-Mary Martin USA

Aptly titled, you won't just be a tourist after reading this book. You'll be greater than a tourist!

-Alan Warner, Grand Rapids, USA

Even though I only have three days to spend in San Miguel in an upcoming visit, I will use the author's suggestions to guide some of my time there. An easy read - with chapters named to guide me in directions I want to go.

 -Robert Catapano, USA

Great insights from a local perspective! Useful information and a very good value!

 -Sarah, USA

This series provides an in-depth experience through the eyes of a local. Reading these series will help you to travel the city in with confidence and it'll make your journey a unique one.

-Andrew Teoh, Ipoh, Malaysia

GREATER THAN A TOURIST- CAIRNS QUEENSLAND AUSTRALIA

50 Travel Tips from a Local

Rachel Caborn

CZYK Publishing Since 2011.
CZYKPublishing.com
Greater Than a Tourist

Mill Hall, PA
All rights reserved.
ISBN: 9798385519330

>TOURIST

50 TRAVEL TIPS FROM A LOCAL

BOOK DESCRIPTION

With travel tips and culture in our guidebooks written by a local, it is never too late to visit Cairns . Greater Than a Tourist - Cairns, Queensland, Australia by author Rachel Caborn offers first-hand and personal insight into the best ways to visit and travel Tropical North Queensland. Most travel books tell you how to travel like a tourist. Although there is nothing wrong with that, as part of the 'Greater Than a Tourist' series, this book will give you candid travel tips from someone who has lived at your next travel destination. This guide book will not tell you exact addresses or store hours but instead gives you knowledge that you may not find in other smaller print travel books. Experience cultural, culinary delights, and attractions with the guidance of a Local. Slow down and get to know the people with this invaluable guide. By the time you finish this book, you will be eager and prepared to discover new activities at your next travel destination.

Inside this travel guide book you will find:
Visitor information from a Local

Tour ideas and inspiration

Valuable guidebook information

Greater Than a Tourist- A Travel Guidebook with 50 Travel Tips from a Local. Slow down, stay in one place, and get to know the people and culture. By the time you finish this book, you will be eager and prepared to travel to your next destination.

OUR STORY

Traveling is a passion of the Greater than a Tourist book series creator. Lisa studied abroad in college, and for their honeymoon Lisa and her husband toured Europe. During her travels to Malta, an older man tried to give her some advice based on his own experience living on the island since he was a young boy. She was not sure if she should talk to the stranger but was interested in his advice. When traveling to some places she was wary to talk to locals because she was afraid that they weren't being genuine. Through her travels, Lisa learned how much locals had to share with tourists. Lisa created the Greater Than a Tourist book series to help connect people with locals. A topic that locals are very passionate about sharing.

TABLE OF CONTENTS

Spots In The City

9. Walk Along The Esplanade

10. Lagoon

11. Night Market

12. Rusty's Market

13. The Pier

14. Botanic Gardens

15. Wildlife Dome

16. Aquarium

17. Art Gallery

18. Coffee

19. Brunch

20. Lunch

21. Dinner

22. Dessert

23. Drinks

24. Dance

Day Trips

25. The Great Barrier Reef

26. Fitzroy Island

Nudey Beach

27. Green Island

28. Port Douglas

29. Kuranda Skyrail

Waterfalls

30. Milla Milla Falls
31. Nandroya Falls
32. Crystal Cascades
33. Windin Falls
34. Babinda Boulders
35. Josephine Falls
36. Behana Gorge
37. Davies Creek
38. Emerald Creek

Walks, Hikes, And Views

39. Mount Bartle Frere
40. Walsh's Pyramid
41. Mamu Tropical Skywalk
42. Campbell's Lookout
43. Lake Barrine

Beaches

44. Trinity Beach
45. Palm Cove
46. Ellis Beach

DEDICATION

This book is dedicated to all the travellers who will start or end their east coast trip in Cairns. No matter how far you've travelled, Cairns will welcome you with open arms. I'd also like to dedicate this book to Justin, who I was able to share and experience this incredible place with.

ABOUT THE AUTHOR

Rachel is a passionate writer and digital marketer from the UK. She left home in 2021 with a one-way plane ticket to Thailand and no idea where she would end up. During her travels, she lived in Cairns for 4 months to work during the Australian winter. During this time, she fell in love with the city and the surrounding areas. Rachel loves exploring new places, you'll find her hiking in the rainforest, reading at the beach, or eating out at local restaurants.

HOW TO USE THIS BOOK

The *Greater Than a Tourist* book series was written by someone who has lived in an area for over three months. The goal of this book is to help travelers either dream or experience different locations by providing opinions from a local. The author has made suggestions based on their own experiences. Please check before traveling to the area in case the suggested places are unavailable.

Travel Advisories: As a first step in planning any trip abroad, check the Travel Advisories for your intended destination.
https://travel.state.gov/content/travel/en/
traveladvisories/traveladvisories.html

FROM THE PUBLISHER

Traveling can be one of the most important parts of a person's life. The anticipation and memories that you have are some of the best. As a publisher of the Greater Than a Tourist, as well as the popular *50 Things to Know* book series, we strive to help you learn about new places, spark your imagination, and inspire you. Wherever you are and whatever you do I wish you safe, fun, and inspiring travel.

Lisa Rusczyk Ed. D.
CZYK Publishing

WELCOME TO
> TOURIST

>TOURIST

All we have to decide is what to
do with the time that is given us

-      J.R.R Tolkien

airns is small in comparison to other Australian cities but that's part of its charm. If you know where to go, you can experience some amazing things and visit some beautiful landscapes. There are waterfalls, beaches, reefs, rainforests, hikes, and a relaxed city life all within a short drive. A visit here will leave you wanting more. Someone once told me that Cairns is the best place in the world. You'll have to see to decide that for yourself.

Cairns
QLD Australia
Climate

	High	Low
January	88	75
February	88	75
March	86	73
April	84	71
May	81	68
June	79	64
July	78	62
August	80	63
September	82	66
October	85	69
November	87	72
December	88	74

GreaterThanaTourist.com

Temperatures are in Fahrenheit degrees.
Source: NOAA

Cairns
Queensland, Australia

1. GETTING AROUND

Cairns is the kind of place where you can effortlessly get around. You can comfortably walk around the centre of Cairns where all the action is. There are plenty of shops and restaurants by the esplanade and dotted around the city all within walking distance. If you're just visiting for a few days then you'll likely be based at a hotel right in the middle of the CBD (central business district). However, one of the reasons that Cairns is so popular is because of its surrounding areas. Just a short drive outside of the CBD will bring you to some completely different and incredible landscapes. That's why if you can bring your car or hire one, you absolutely should.

Car hire in Cairns is very common, there are plenty of places to choose from around the city. Usually, you can show up on the day and hire one then and there, but in the busy peak season, it's a good idea to book in advance. You can rent a car for just a day trip or the entire duration of your stay. Plan your activities in advance so you know when you'll need to rent a vehicle and when you can use public transport. Parking in the city is free in most places and there are also a few paid car parks. Typically, you can easily find a free spot right in the CBD, but at peak times when it's busier, you're better off heading straight to a paid car park or parking a little further out.

There are no trains, metros, or trams in Cairns but there is an extensive bus network. Many places just outside of the city can be reached by bus, but a lot of the waterfalls and hikes are only accessible with your own vehicle. If you do want to travel anywhere by bus, then you'll need cash in small change. At the time of writing this, you can't pay by card. Elsewhere in Queensland, such as in Brisbane, public transport like buses is paid for with a Translink Go card. This won't work in Cairns, although I suspect it will change in future. For now, you're best to get some coins ready before you get on the bus. You can ask the bus driver for a ticket, just let them know where you are going and if you need a single or return ticket. I found the best way of navigating the buses in Cairns is to simply use Google Maps.

If you want to reach some places outside of the city where the buses don't go, and you don't want to hire a car, then a tour group might be for you. Tours such as Uncle Brian's Tours are a great way to see lots of the surrounding areas without having to navigate them yourself. This particular tour is especially popular with backpackers. There are a couple of different tours that will take you to either the Rainforest or to Cape Tribulation in a jam-packed 1 or 2-day trip.

If you are staying further out of the CBD and need to get a taxi, there are a few options to choose from in Cairns. There are plenty of taxi ranks all over the CBD where you can join the queue and taxis will come, but one of the best options is to call Cairns Taxis directly. To avoid waiting around, call and book a taxi in advance. I love using Uber at home and when I travel, however, I would avoid Uber and stick to booking in advance with the local taxi company.

Across Australian cities, you will find beam electric scooters and bikes. This is a fun way to get around the city and helpful if you want to quickly get from A to B without walking in the Australian sun. I'd recommend taking a beam scooter from the esplanade up to the botanic gardens. You'll get a lovely view from the esplanade without the long walk in the heat. To use the beam scooters in Cairns, you'll need to download the Beam app. Make sure you wear your helmet and pay attention to where you are allowed to ride. Otherwise have a fun time scooting by the sea!

Cairns Esplanade

2. SUN PROTECTION

One of the most important things you must be prepared for when visiting Cairns is the Australian sun. The sun here is like no other and if you're prone to sunburn be very careful. Australia has some of the highest UV indices in the world because the country is closer to the equator than most.

When visiting Cairns always wear sunscreen no matter what, even if it looks cloudy outside. Trust me, I'm telling you from experience. Even if you're not someone who burns, please apply sunscreen to protect yourself from UV rays. Always carry sunscreen on you especially if you are doing a day trip somewhere, as you will need to reapply throughout the day. Choose factor 50 as a minimum, anything else won't withstand the Australian sun. You should opt for a reef-safe sunscreen and apply it at least 30 minutes before getting in the ocean.

As well as wearing sunscreen there are some other things you can do to help you survive, and thrive, in the Aussie sunshine. Stay in the shade when you can. You may enjoy sunbathing on your usual holidays but in Australia try shade bathing, your skin will thank you later. Take a parasol to the beach when you can, and choose a spot beneath the trees. Drink plenty of water throughout the day, staying hydrated is key. Wear clothes to cover your skin for added sun protection. Consider investing in a rash vest or also known as a rashy if you plan on swimming or snorkelling a lot. You'll likely know all of this already, but I want to stress the importance of looking after yourself in the sun and how to avoid heat stroke or sunburn.

3. OCEAN AWARE

Before you get in the ocean be prepared and aware of what could be in there. North Queensland waters are infested with crocodiles. Yes, you read that right. There are crocodiles in many rivers and even sometimes in the ocean. Beaches will have signposts to let you know if there are crocs here and when to keep your eyes out for them. Any bodies of water will usually have signs to say if they are safe to swim or not. There are plenty of creeks and waterfalls around the area that are free from crocs. As a general rule of thumb, don't swim in rivers and only swim in the lifeguarded areas at the beach.

It's not just crocs you'll need to watch out for in the ocean, you'll need to be mindful of stingers. Jellyfish inhabit North Queensland oceans in the warmer months from November to March. In the cooler months, you'll generally be safe from stingers but in the summer months, it's essential to wear a stinger suit when swimming in the sea. There will be signs at the beach to explain this to you so make sure you check before going in the water. Even though the stinger season is from November to March, sometimes they arrive earlier so it's always a good idea to check what others are doing in the water. Locals are usually the first to spot when the stingers have arrived, so if you see people in stinger suits then that's your sign.

Many popular beaches will have a stinger net and lifeguard present. These nets make swimming much safer but be warned, not all stingers are stopped by the nets. Very small jellyfish can bypass the net and if you are stung by one it can have a fatal impact. It's also useful to note that crocs aren't stopped by stinger nets either, but when there is a lifeguard present it will be safer.

Hopefully I haven't scared you too much, but it's important to know what you're in for before you go for a swim. If in doubt, swim at your hotel swimming pool, the Cairns lagoon, or venture out to a waterfall for stinger and croc-free waters.

4. CHOOSE YOUR SEASON

When you choose to visit Cairns will significantly impact your experience there. There are only two seasons, the wet season from November to March, and the dry season from April to October. I lived in Cairns from July to September and can safely say around this time is the best time to visit. As the rest of the country is in winter, it's no surprise that these months are also the peak tourist time. I still think it's the best time to visit because it's sunny most of the time and rarely rains. In these months, temperatures are around a comfortable 78 degrees Fahrenheit, unlike the 86+ degrees in the summer months.

If you decide to visit during the rainy season then be prepared for rain like you have never seen before. It rains a lot and it might disrupt your plans like visiting the beach or hiking in the rainforest. One of the benefits of visiting in the rainy season is waterfalls get stronger and bigger and you'll likely have them to yourself.

5. WHERE TO STAY

There are plenty of places to stay in Cairns as it's geared up for tourists. Choose from 5-star hotels or budget hostels, there's a wide range for all price points. If you are travelling in peak tourist times, you should book your accommodation in advance as they do sell out quickly. Hostels tend to up their rates in peak season and depending on how busy it is. However, they sometimes do better long-term deals when you book in person. There are lots of places to book accommodation, Booking.com, Agoda and Hostelworld are just a few.

Let's start with some of the best and most popular hotels in Cairns. Located by the marina, the Shangri-La is surrounded by restaurants and bars with easy access to tours to The Great Barrier Reef and just a short stroll away from Cairns CBD. The rooms are modern and sophisticated, there is a luxurious outdoor pool, three bars and restaurants to choose from.

The Novotel Cairns Oasis Resort is the only place you'll find a swim-up bar in Cairns. Located by the esplanade in the CBD, they have a large outdoor pool area and an extensive restaurant. The facilities are modern and spacious, ideal for any type of stay.

There are three Crystalbrook hotels in Cairns, Riley, Flynn, and Bailey. These are located in the CBD near the esplanade each with restaurants, bars, and pools. You'll thoroughly enjoy your stay at a Crystalbrook hotel with modern rooms and all the amenities you would need. The Crystalbrook Riley has a glorious outdoor pool, the Crystralbrook Flynn has a large bar area with live music and DJs, and the Crystalbrook Bailey is modern and artistic, decorated with Australian art.

Moving onto some of the hostels, I'll start with the most well-known hostel in Cairns and perhaps the most notorious in all of Australia. Gilligan's is known for being a party hostel as it's also a nightclub. If you want to go out, be social and party during your time in Cairns, then Gilligan's is the hostel for you. If you can, try to get a room facing the road rather than the club so it's a bit quieter when you eventually do want to sleep. Aside from being a party hostel, the facilities are nice and there is a large pool area outside.

Mad Monkey is a popular hostel chain across Australia and Asia. There are three Mad Monkey Hostels in Cairns: Central, Waterfront, and Village. Central is the most popular for backpackers visiting short term, there are plenty of communal areas and a pool area. Waterfront is in the best location on the esplanade but it is one of the smallest hostels in Cairns. Village is popular with long-term stays as it's slightly further out but has good facilities and a community feel.

Global Backpackers is located on the esplanade near the lagoon with a communal balcony area that overlooks the ocean. It's a social but quiet hostel which is a great middle ground if you want to meet others but won't be up all night partying.

YHA hostels are popular all over Australia and you can sometimes get deals when you bulk-book them for your trip. Cairns Central YHA is a quieter hostel in

Cairns but it still has a social atmosphere with nice facilities.

Bounce is a popular choice for many visiting Cairns. It's a social hostel with a modest pool area, good beds, and clean facilities.

These hotels and hostels are just a few popular ones to get you started on your search for accommodation, but the city has plenty more options to choose from.

6. GET TO KNOW THE AUSSIE WAY

When you land in Australia you'll likely be met with a few phrases and things that you've never seen or heard of before. You'll most definitely be greeted at the airport with a "G'day mate", but what if I told you there's something Aussies say far more often? Let me share some of the Aussie lingo and things around you'll likely encounter when you visit Cairns.

What do the locals say more than "G'day mate"? They say "How's it going?" If an Aussie asks you "How's it going?" that's their way of saying Hey! This is a common phrase and you'll likely hear it a lot. If you want to get into the Aussie spirit use this as a greeting and you won't go wrong.

You've probably heard of this one before, Aussies refer to their flip-flops as thongs. There's more to thongs than you might think. The Aussie way of life is a shoe-free way of life. Most Aussies you'll meet will be barefoot or wearing thongs as the bare minimum. Don't be surprised if you see people wandering around the supermarkets barefoot, that's completely normal in Australia. Something I was a little surprised to see at first (if you've ever been to the UK you'll know it's far too cold and wet to be barefoot anywhere!) Some places like restaurants require you to wear shoes so always pack your thongs just in case you plan on embracing being barefoot.

One thing you will see when visiting Cairns and the surrounding area is bush turkeys. They are everywhere in the wild, if you go for a hike or a walk in the rainforest expect to see them wandering around. Another bird you might come across is Curlews. You'll notice these birds by their long thin legs. They run around in the centre of Cairns, usually in the early morning or late in the evening. You might even hear a screaming noise at night, especially if you stay further out of the city, which will likely just be the Curlews. They are noisy birds for sure!

Something more harmful than bush turkeys and Curlews is snakes. It's true, there are many dangerous snakes in Australia and particularly in Tropical North Queensland. Realistically you won't see any in the city of Cairns, but if you decide to venture out to visit some waterfalls or do a bush walk then you might come into contact with them. Just watch where you are walking and you'll be fine.

7. LEARN THE ABORIGINAL HISTORY AND CULTURE

Learning about indigenous history and aboriginal culture is an essential activity when visiting Australia. It's one of the first things you should do when you arrive in the country to fully understand the history and how it impacts the country today. Cairns is a starting point for many when visiting Australia so it's a great place to get started with your aboriginal education.

One of the things you might notice when visiting is that before events, talks, tours or meetings take place there will be an Acknowledgement of County speech to pay respect to the traditional owners of the land. Once you understand the history this will make much more sense.

There are a few aboriginal tours that will take you outside and around Cairns to learn about the history and the land. Some notable places to visit are the Daintree Rainforest, Mossman Gorge, and the closest to Cairns, Kuranda. In Kuranda, you can take part in the Rainforestation Experience where you'll watch an Aboriginal dance performance and go on a Dreamtime Walk to learn about the land and history. You'll find some activities offer bundle tickets so if you're interested in the Rainforestation Experience you can also get a ticket to include the Kuranda Skyrail, which I'll touch on more later.

8. WHERE TO SHOP

When you arrive in Cairns, and throughout Australia in general, it's useful to know where to shop for groceries and other essentials. Coles and Woolworths are the two main supermarkets where you'll find all your typical groceries. If you want to buy alcohol then you'll need to visit one of the liquor stores. These are usually next door to supermarkets, and you'll find a few dotted around the CBD. Look for Liquorland or BWS. Cairns Central is the main shopping centre just a short walk from Cairns CBD. Here, you'll find just about all the shops you could need during your stay in Cairns including clothing stores, a pharmacy and a food hall. Kmart is a useful store to know as it has pretty much anything you might need such as swimwear, shoes, camping equipment, eskies, games and tech. There are plenty of tourist souvenir shops by the esplanade if you're looking for a gift or something to take home with you. There are also many stalls in the Night Market that you'll want to check out, but we'll talk more about that later.

SPOTS IN THE CITY

9. WALK ALONG THE ESPLANADE

Walking along the esplanade is one of my absolute favourite things to do in Cairns. I can visit time and time again and still love it just as much as the first time I visited. The view changes almost every time you visit, depending on the tides and the weather so revisit the esplanade during your stay in Cairns. The landscape from the esplanade is just incredible, especially when the tide is in. You can see the ocean by your feet and the mountains in the distance. You might even spot a pelican or two if you're lucky. If you can muster up an early morning to walk along the boardwalk before a day of activities, then you absolutely should. It's much quieter, calmer, and not to mention, much cooler first thing in the morning. You should return to visit the esplanade in the evening to watch the sunset before heading out to dinner. Sunsets in Cairns are beautiful when the sky is clear, and sitting by the sea makes them even better.

Cairns Esplanade

10. LAGOON

The Cairns Lagoon is a popular spot to spend the day or an afternoon relaxing. It's completely free so a great option if you are on a budget, and perfect if your accommodation doesn't have a swimming pool. Part of the experience of being on holiday in the tropics is to relax and enjoy the sunshine, so you should do exactly that. The lagoon is located right on the esplanade so you're never far from anything you might need, like shops or restaurants. There are plenty of places to sit with showers and toilets close by. The lagoon is family-friendly, and there is always a lifeguard on duty, from early in the morning until late in the evening. There are even outdoor BBQ tables, which you will see all over Australia. Aussies love to cook a BBQ outside with friends and family, so grab some food, and utensils, and get that shrimp on the barbie! There's plenty of grass surrounding the lagoon so it's a perfect place for a picnic too. The lagoon overlooks the ocean which makes it another great place to be when the sun sets. I've also been told the lagoon is a fantastic place to be when it starts raining since you're already in the water. For that one, you'll have to let me know. Next door to the lagoon is the Cairns wheel, where you can go to get an even better view of Cairns and the sea. I'd suggest a visit to the wheel at sunset since I think this is the most beautiful time of day in Cairns.

11. NIGHT MARKET

On one of your evenings in Cairns, you must visit the Night Market. After 4 pm the Night Market comes alive every day with a variety of stalls opening up. It's indoors so you won't have to worry if there's a downpour. You'll find a wide range of food on offer and all sorts of things being sold. There is a Thai food buffet, Vietnamese street food, sushi, fish and chips, just to name a few things. It's a relaxed environment to grab a casual bite to eat. The food is well-priced and good value for money, it's relatively cheap compared to some of the restaurants nearby. A top tip, if you go much later in the evening then some of the food is discounted. Check both entrances to the Night Market as there are food places on both sides. You'll also find a range of stalls inside selling all kinds of things like massages, stickers, souvenirs, Aussie hats and my personal favourite, homemade banana bread. Every time I visited the Night Market (which was a fair few times) I would buy a different loaf because they were just so good. They do vegan loaves and different flavours like fruits and nuts, which I'd highly recommend. There are plenty of options for dessert in and around the night market too.

12. RUSTY'S MARKET

Another great but very different market to visit in Cairns is Rusty's Market. Picture a farmers market and that's pretty much what Rusty's Market is. This market is only on from Friday to Sunday from 5 am to 6 pm, and 3 pm on Sundays. It's located in the CBD on Grafton Street. You'll want to turn up as early as you can to get the best pick of the bunch. Imagine all the fresh fruit and veg locally grown and harvested and that's exactly what you'll find. Enjoy what this farmers market has to offer and take advantage of the exotic fruits you can find in the tropics. The colourful fruit and veg will draw you in but you'll stay for the wide variety of offerings inside. Grab a coffee and a pastry, pick up some cakes, browse the clothes and marvel at the art. Chat with the locals and see what's good. Sugar cane juice is a popular favourite.

13. THE PIER

Walk down the esplanade towards the lagoon and keep going then, you'll reach Cairns pier. This is a great spot for shopping as there are some unique boutiques and local shops. You'll find plenty of restaurants and bars around this area too which are well worth a visit on one of your evenings in Cairns. If you're a seafood lover then definitely check out Tha Fish, their creative dishes can be enjoyed with a beautiful view overlooking the marina. Vitalia's Italian Restaurant is a popular choice in Cairns for its authentic pizza and pasta. There's The Pier Bar where tourists and locals alike gather for a relaxed drink at the end of the week. I'd also recommend Howlin Jays for a quirky cocktail experience in an American Diner-style setting with a serving of wings and fries.

14. BOTANIC GARDENS

If you want to escape the city for a bit of flora and fauna, without venturing too far, then the Botanic Gardens is the perfect place. There are plenty of buses from the city, or you can take a slightly longer walk right from the end of the esplanade. Another great idea is to hire a bicycle and cycle to and around the gardens. The Botanic Gardens are small but provide a lovely little walk amongst some beautiful tropical plants and flowers. The tropical boardwalk gives the feel of walking in the rainforest amongst some of these native plants. The gardens are free to enter and make a great picnic spot, there's also a little cafe on site too. There's a conservatory where you'll spot some colourful butterflies and they even host guided walks around the garden. Visit early to enjoy a stroll around without the intense midday sun.

15. WILDLIFE DOME

A rainy day in Cairns is best spent at the Cairns ZOOM and Wildlife Dome. It's a great place to take the whole family as kids will particularly love this activity. As you would expect, the Wildlife Dome is home to some native Australian animals, it's like Cairns's very own mini zoo. You can see koalas, crocodiles, cockatoos, and snakes. They hold talks throughout the day so you can learn all about these native Aussie animals. A great tip is to arrive in the morning and get your ticket. Then you can see what time the talks are on throughout the day and dip in and out of the dome at the times that best suit you. As well as animals the dome is a unique experience in Cairns because of the ZOOM activities. There are high ropes, zip lines, beams, and climbing walls. They even have a Dome Climb activity where you can scale the outside of the dome. It's a thrilling activity that kids of all ages, and even adults, will enjoy.

16. AQUARIUM

Another great indoor activity that is perfect for families is the Cairns Aquarium. There is an extensive collection of marine life that can help you learn about Queensland waters. There's plenty to see and you can easily spend a few hours exploring the different exhibits. It's a great idea to visit the Aquarium early on during your trip to Cairns and before you head out to The Great Barrier Reef. That way, you can understand a bit more about what you're seeing when you arrive at the reef. Try a guided tour to learn more and hear about the Aquarium's conservation efforts. The Aquarium also has touch pools so you can get up close and personal with some of the aquatic life. For an alternative experience, visit the Aquarium at twilight or dine in their very own restaurant.

17. ART GALLERY

Continuing on the theme of rainy day activities (because you might need them) Cairns Art Gallery is the perfect place. This is one of the first places I visited in Cairns because, of course, there was a torrential downpour the first day I arrived. It's a modest little free art gallery that packs a punch. Although small, and if raining outside it will likely be busy, it's home to some interesting and impressive art. The exhibits change frequently so there's always something new to see. During your visit, you can also stop by Perrotta's at the Gallery for some Italian brunch, lunch, or dinner. I visited for brunch and it's a lovely little restaurant with outdoor seating serving delicious food.

Where To Eat And Drink

18. COFFEE

Australians take their coffee seriously, so let's take a look at some of the best spots in Cairns for your morning coffee.

At Wharf One Cafe, have your morning coffee overlooking the Cairns marina. This might be one of the best views in the city served with locally roasted coffee. They also have a great menu if you're feeling peckish.

Perhaps the best place to buy plants in Cairns is Succulicing & Co, but they serve excellent coffee too. Sit down in this cosy plant haven and enjoy your morning coffee surrounded by the greenery of exotic plants. It's a little slice of tropical heaven in the Cairns CBD.

Literally a cosy nook in the centre of Cairns, The Nook is an intimate and quaint spot for a coffee catch-up. Keep an eye out for the community chess set and make your move.

A good all-rounder, Bang & Grind on Spencer Street is a great option for your morning coffee before a day of activities. There are also plenty of breakfast options to fuel you for the day.

If you're outside of the city, perhaps on route to visit some waterfalls for the day, stop by Whitfield and visit The Nest. You can feel like a local out in the suburbs around Cairns and this is a cute little gem of a coffee shop to try.

19. BRUNCH

I personally love going for brunch so here are some of my top recommendations in Cairns. The perfect brunch spot for your favourite breakfast foods, The Chambers is one of the best and most popular brunch spots in town. Choose between smoothie bowls, smashed avo, french toast, you name it. They also do fantastic cocktails if you're in the mood for a boozy brunch.

Caffined on Grafton Street is sure to provide great coffee and great food. They pride themselves on their locally sourced seasonal ingredients. Order the popular Caffined Chili Eggs and a Dirty Chai Latte.

A little outside of the CBD towards the end of the esplanade, you'll find Guyala Cafe. This is a popular spot with locals as the food and service are top-tier. It's a beautiful cafe with indoor and outdoor seating and you can really feel the attention to detail in their dishes.

If you're in the mood for something sweet then Waffle On Cairns is the place to go. They have a huge menu of sweet and savoury waffle varieties as well as plenty of other breakfast options.

As I mentioned, Perrotta's at the Gallery is another good choice for brunch. Rusty's Market is also a great place to grab breakfast but go early.

20. LUNCH

If you're spending a day in the city then here are some lunch places for you to check out. Located on the esplanade by the Lagoon is Lemoncello's Cairns. It's a small but intimate, casual place to enjoy some amazing Italian food. It's popular with tourists and locals alike so don't be surprised if they are fully booked. They are open for lunch and dinner so opt for lunch if you want to avoid booking ahead. On the menu, you'll find fresh pasta, authentic Italian pizzas, and some of the best seafood in town.

Hailed as the best spot in Cairns for ramen, Ganbaranba is the place to go to get a slice of Japanese food. This place smells amazing when you walk in, and in the evenings you'll likely see a queue outside. You can choose how you like your noodles (soft, medium, or hard) and enjoy them with some iced tea which is much needed in the Cairns heat. The gyoza is also particularly popular here so get a portion on the side.

If you're in the mood for an easy-going burger then head to Grill'd. This Australian burger chain makes some of the best burgers around for a quick chilled lunch or dinner. I used to work at Grill'd in Cairns and I'd always have their impossible (meat-free) burgers on my lunch break. These veggie burgers are just so good, I'd highly recommend to any vegetarians or vegans as they have a wide range of tasty options.

Lemoncello's Cairns

21. DINNER

There are several places to dine in Cairns, you will be spoilt for choice. Let me share some top recommendations if you are struggling to decide. If you're looking for a fine dining experience during your visit to Cairns, then head to Tamarind, located in The Reef Hotel Casino. They've won many awards for their Australian freestyle dishes, and are highly regarded by locals and tourists. There's plenty to choose from on the menu which is served with a wide drinks menu. Bookings are essential.

Edge Hill is a suburb in Cairns that is home to both the Botanic Gardens and a handful of amazing restaurants. NOA is a popular hit with the locals for its tapas dishes and signature cocktails. It's also a great place to visit for brunch.

Ochre Restaurant is one of the most highly awarded restaurants in Cairns. The menu serves fresh Australian produce with a view overlooking the waterfront. Try the 6-course degustation menu for a real tasting experience. Remember to book in advance.

Enjoy authentic Vietnamese food at Pho Viet Vietnamese. You can expect a relaxed environment just as if you were eating in Vietnam. It's cosy and small so perfect for a couple or small group. I loved this place, there are lots on the menu, the food tastes great and it's affordable.

A popular spot on the esplanade, Villa Romana Trattoria serves up delicious Italian food throughout the day. It's in the perfect location close to many hotels and has a great view during the day time. Choose one of their wood-fired pizzas for a real taste of Naples.

The Night Market and The Pier are great options for dinner too.

22. DESSERT

With all the delicious options in Cairns, you'll find it difficult to skip dessert. Right outside of the Night Market, you'll find Churro Time, the place to go for your sweet tooth fix. I'd recommend choosing the churros and ice cream and then sit by the esplanade to watch the sunset *chefs kiss*.

There are a few gelato places in Cairns so it's only right you visit at least one of them. Just Devine Gelato is close to the esplanade and has a wide variety to choose from. Definitely, the place to stop in the evening on the way back to your hotel.

YOMG (Yo My Goodness) is a frozen yoghurt place with a twist. You can completely customise your dessert by choosing your flavour of frozen yoghurt and toppings. It's located just opposite the Night Market and there's something for everyone here. Pro tip: start small when filling your cup and leave plenty of space for toppings.

23. DRINKS

After enjoying the flavours of Cairns, head for some celebratory drinks. Flamingos is the speciality cocktail bar you need to visit when you're feeling fancy. It's very small and intimate but it's a great atmosphere with incredibly fun cocktails. It can get pretty busy in here so stop by early in the evening to grab a seat. It's on the pricey side but worth at least one fun drink in this environment.

Salt House is a great spot for both dinner and drinks. There is plenty of outdoor seating including comfy seats and day beds. It's a perfect place for a couple of drinks to catch up with friends. They usually have a good DJ playing to create a fun and chilled vibe. If you're on a budget then check out the place on a Monday night for good deals on drinks.

24. DANCE

Dance the night away in one of the various clubs in Cairns. Gilligan's is perhaps the biggest club in Cairns and a rite of passage for backpackers visiting the city. They have a few different rooms with different styles of music and themed nights throughout the week. You can expect to find DJs visiting the city and playing at Gilligan's, but they also have live music and bands playing too.

New to the scene, Cairns Dirty Laundry is a lively club with a fun laundromat theme. Slide down the Laundry chute to get to the club and dance the night away.

If you're looking for somewhere else to dance then head to Woolshed. It's much smaller than the other clubs but just as energetic and crazy. It can get pretty busy on the weekend but still has a laidback feel.

The Cairns Party Bus is one for the party backpackers out there. It's a fun way to meet other travellers and visit a few different bars around the city. It's rowdy, loud and exciting but that's all part of the fun. I can almost guarantee you won't find any locals here though.

DAY TRIPS

25. THE GREAT BARRIER REEF

The main reason most tourists visit Cairns is to visit The Great Barrier Reef. It's without a doubt the most popular thing to do here, and an absolute must during your trip to Cairns. If you only visit for a couple of days, make visiting The Great Barrier Reef your number one priority.

The Great Barrier Reef itself stretches from right at the top of the Australian east coast in Cape York, down to Bundaberg down south. You can do tours and trips in different places along this coastline. Some popular spots include Port Douglas, just north of Cairns, and around the Whitsundays islands, from Airlie Beach. You might decide to visit The Great Barrier Reef in more than one place, as there are different areas of the reef to explore. I've snorkelled in a few spots along the coast and the experiences have been different each time. I would highly recommend doing a dedicated day trip in Cairns, it's the most popular spot to visit The

Great Barrier Reef as there are tours setting off every day.

There are several different tours and trips you can take, from scenic flights to liveaboard diving trips. You can choose whatever type of activity appeals most to you. If you're not sure where to begin I would suggest choosing a snorkelling day tour. You get to snorkel at a few different spots around the reef and have plenty of time throughout the day to relax on the boat. Snorkelling is an ideal way to see the reef as you don't need much, or any experience, compared to diving. Most of the snorkelling sites have shallow reefs, so you can see enough without needing to dive down. On these trips, they often have the option to upgrade to diving. This is a great opportunity for first-time divers to complete an introductory dive and try it out, whilst still having plenty of time to snorkel. These types of trips are great if you have people in your group who want to snorkel and others who want to dive. You can all go together and enjoy the experience even whilst doing different things.

If you're not overly confident in the water, then consider a snorkel and scenic flight trip. The snorkelling will allow you to get up close to the reef as

I would highly recommend you get into the water if you can. The crew on board can usually support you with flotation devices and life jackets so you're able to feel more confident while swimming. The scenic flight is a great option if you don't want to spend all the time in the water, but it also provides a different perspective of the reef which is amazing in itself. There are other trips available for more advanced divers who are keen to spend all their time diving in the reef. Whatever your preference and budget allows, there is a trip for you. The Great Barrier Reef will likely be the highlight of your visit to Cairns, you'll see the most amazing things and have the best day.

26. FITZROY ISLAND

Just off the coast of Cairns, there are a few islands you can visit. One of which is Fitzroy Island which you can reach in 45 minutes by ferry. It's well worth dedicating a full day of your trip to Cairns to visiting this island. Fitzroy Island is known for its amazing snorkelling and beautiful coral beaches. Just off the main beach where you arrive, there is a fantastic snorkelling spot. You'll see a big large white rock, conveniently named 'White Rock', and that's where you'll want to head. When I snorkelled here, I saw so many huge green turtles, a reef shark, as well as various fish and coral. I was mind-blown! Fitzroy Island is up there with one of the best places I've snorkelled so far. It is, after all, still a part of The Great Barrier Reef. If you love snorkelling you'll want to spend a while here. Then you can take the 20 minute walk to Nudey Beach. This is not a nudest beach as the name might suggest, it's just a beautiful white coral beach which has previously won awards for being one of the best beaches in Australia. The waters are clear, warm and good for snorkelling. On the way back to the ferry, you can stop off at Foxy's bar for a drink overlooking the ocean. If you have more time and wanted to explore the rest of the island, you can hike up to the top for some impressive views. Be warned that this is a long walk that can be difficult in the heat, so if you want to hike do it in the morning when you first arrive. There's also a turtle rehabilitation centre on the island where you can see many turtles and learn more about them. If you did want to spend more time on the island there is a hotel and a campground.

Nudey Beach

27. GREEN ISLAND

If you want to spend more time on the islands, relaxing on the beach and snorkelling, then visit Green Island. The ferry will take you 45 minutes and you can spend just the morning or the whole day here. There's more coral at Fitzroy Island, as the floor at Green Island is lined with seagrass. However, this makes it an attractive spot for sea turtles. There are often daily sightings of sea turtles, particularly in the morning. Snorkel around the pier and keep your eyes open, you can even see reef sharks and sting rays. There's a short boardwalk on the island too that will take you through the greenery of the national park to another beach on the island. If you wanted to stay longer on Green Island, check yourself into the Green Island Resort.

28. PORT DOUGLAS

Another popular day trip just outside of Cairns is to visit Port Douglas. Many visitors will stay in Port Douglas, but I think you can experience and explore most of the area in just a day trip if you didn't have time to stay longer. You'll likely want to hire a car, or bring your own, to have the flexibility of exploring the area. The drive to Port Douglas from Cairns will take about an hour along the Captain Cook highway, perhaps one of the most picturesque roads in Australia. Although it's only an hour away, you should allow much more time as you'll want to make some stops en route.

The first place you should stop is Rex Lookout for an incredible view of the beach. You might even see some paragliders as this is a popular spot for them. Further north on your drive is Pretty Beach, an idyllic untouched spot if you're looking for a more secluded spot. There are also many lovely beachside camp spots along the way to Port Douglas.

When you arrive in Port Douglas, you should have some lunch at one of the many cafes along the main street. It's a laidback place so take time to relax after the drive. Check out Trinity Bay Lookout for an incredible view of Four Mile Beach. This beach is a wide long beach with plenty of space to unwind in the afternoon. As it's Port Douglas's main beach, it can get quite busy at peak times. Lastly, you'll want to visit Rex Smeal Park, this is an ideal place to watch the sunset with incredible views out to the ocean. They also have a popular campsite here. A day trip to Port Douglas will guarantee some amazing views and beaches, as well as time to sit back and relax.

Thala Beach Nature Reserve

29. KURANDA SKYRAIL

A popular activity in Cairns is to go on the Skyrail and visit Kuranda. This experience allows you to walk through the rainforest and see it from different perspectives, as well as visit the quirky town of Kuranda and everything it has to offer. This is a great family-friendly activity that everyone can enjoy. I would recommend this to people who perhaps are not keen on hiking in the rainforest but still want to be immersed in it. The walks are short and relatively accessible, compared to visiting many of the other waterfalls in the area.

You should book your tickets in advance using the website as the spots fill up quickly, particularly for the Scenic Railway. You'll need to select time slots for your departure and return from Kuranda when booking your ticket. Consider what you might want to see and do while in Kuranda to ensure you have plenty of time during your visit.

If you have a vehicle you can drive straight to the Skyrail start point, which is about 15 minutes outside of Cairns. Only drive yourself if you are planning on getting the Skyrail return rather than the Scenic railway back. Otherwise, you can get an additional bus pick-up from Cairns CBD. This is the starting point of the Skyrail cableway that takes you to Kuranda. There are a number of stops along the way where you can walk along the boardwalks in the rainforest and see Barron Falls. You can visit this waterfall separately from the Skyrail but it's not one you can swim in. There are plenty of information boards to explain what you see as you walk around, or you can join one of the guided tours. When you get on and off the cablecars, you have as much or as little time as you wish to explore before going to your next stop.

At the end of the Skyrail, you'll come to the quirky town of Kuranda. This is a great time to have some lunch and wander around the town exploring the local shops. In Kuranda, they have many other activities such as the Koala Gardens, Australian Butterfly Sanctuary, Birdworld, and the Rainforestation Experience.

On your return to Cairns, you can either take the Skyrail back or go via the Scenic Railway which will bring you to Cairns Central Railway Station. You can swap the journey and do the Scenic Railway first but you would need to go to Freshwater Railway to depart rather than Cairns CBD, which likely won't be as easy for you. The Scenic Railway is exactly as it sounds, a leisurely 2-hour train journey through the rainforest from Kuranda to Cairns.

>TOURIST

WATERFALLS

30. MILLA MILLA FALLS

Tropical North Queensland is home to many waterfalls which you can access just a short drive away from Cairns. It's one of the many charms of the area and something you should definitely make time for during your trip. If you're visiting for a few days, try and make one of them a day trip to some of the main waterfalls. If you have more time, dedicate 2 or 3 days to waterfall hopping, depending on how much you like hiking and swimming. There is an abundance of waterfalls to choose from and I think I've visited almost all of them. I'll help you understand the differences between them so you can pick the best ones to visit. I've only noted waterfalls accessible with a 2WD as most tourists won't have access to a 4WD when they visit.

Keep in mind that the waterfalls may look different to the pictures you've seen, depending on the amount of rainfall there has been. I visited most of these falls during the summer and they still all had a pretty good flow of water from them, unlike some other falls I visited further down south of the east coast where the water had completely dried up. From my experience, Barron Falls looks much more impressive after heavy rainfall, and so does Milla Milla, but they are still worth visiting in the drier months.

Whilst we are on the topic of rainfall, when the falls are more powerful they are more dangerous. Always be careful before getting in the water as sometimes the currents can be too strong which can be fatal. You might have seen someone swimming in a certain area in a photo, but on the day you're swimming there, it might not be as safe. Always keep an eye out for any safety signs as they will tell you where it's safe to swim.

Milla Milla Falls is probably the most famous and iconic waterfall in Australia so it's well worth the visit. If you've seen Peter Andre's Mysterious Girl music video, or a Herbal Essence advert, then you'll recognise Milla Milla Falls. The drive from Cairns will take about an hour and 45 minutes. You can park right next to the falls so there's no walking required, just a couple of steps down to the water. The falls go into an open swimming hole so there's ample space to swim. There's a public toilet and plenty of grass surrounding the falls for a picnic. Milla Milla Falls is part of the Atherton Tablelands waterfall circuit, so you can see more waterfalls in this area on the drive.

Milla Milla Falls

31. NANDROYA FALLS

One of the other waterfalls in the Atherton Tablelands waterfall circuit is Nandroya Falls. This is one of my personal favourites as you get really immersed in the rainforest and it feels like you've gone off the beaten track, unlike Milla Milla Falls which is a tourist hotspot. To get to Nandroya Falls head to Henrietta Creek Campground to park then take the 3.5km hike to get to the falls. You'll pass the smaller Silver Falls and some creeks along the walk. The walk isn't too steep and you're surrounded by the rainforest along the track. It tends to be quiet there and feels very secluded. You'll likely have the falls all to yourself where you can relax and swim. Tchupala Falls and Wallicher Falls are two other waterfalls very close by with a similar feel but a shorter walk.

32. CRYSTAL CASCADES

The Crystal Cascades is the closest waterfall to Cairns about 25 minutes away from the city, but that also makes it the busiest especially on weekends when locals visit. It's great for swimming as there's a large open pool at the bottom of the falls. There are a few different areas along the stream which also make for great swimming spots when it's a little crowded in the main pool. There is a short 1.2km walk to the falls which is fairly well paved. This easy walk makes it a great place for groups and families to visit. I found the water at the Crystal Cascades slightly warmer than some of the other falls I've visited, perhaps because it's more open but all freshwater falls are a little chilly even in the summer! The Crystal Cascades is one of a few waterfalls around Cairns where you can do canyoneering, as well as at Behana Gorge.

33. WINDIN FALLS

Windin Falls provides, what I think, is one of the best views from a waterfall. Rather than visiting the bottom of the waterfall like the last two I mentioned, when you go to Windin Falls you'll walk all the way to the top. Now the 11km round hike to the top of Windin Falls is not for the faint-hearted. It might be a little difficult if you're not an avid walker but it's absolutely worth it. You'll want to start in the morning early to avoid the heat and the crowds, it's a popular spot to visit and there's not much space up there for lots of people. An extra bonus for going early in the morning, is the incredible sounds of the rainforest you'll hear. There are so many unique birds it's fascinating to be immersed in.

Once you get to the end of the walk, you'll arrive at the top of the waterfall where you can see the water dropping down and the incredible views looking out into the valley between the mountains. The view itself is absolutely jaw-dropping. Depending on what the water is like, you can actually swim in the little infinity pool at the top. But please, please, be careful if you decide to swim and only enter the water at your own risk! Otherwise, just take in the incredible views and have a snack to prepare for the walk back. I actually saw a Red-bellied black snake across the path on my visit here, which is a venomous snake. I waited for the snake to move and proceeded on the walk. As I mentioned before, you might encounter snakes when you venture into the bush but don't worry just watch where you are going and keep to the path.

Windin Falls

34. BABINDA BOULDERS

Taking a U-turn from Windin Falls, Babinda Boulders is a much more accessible swimming hole to visit. I'd say there are two parts to Babinda Boulders, there is the incredible views of the water rolling over the large boulders and the large natural swimming pool. You can park right next to the swimming area which is large and open. It's probably the largest, flattest swimming hole in the area. Many people take floaties here as there's not much of a current at all, it's more like a creek than the other waterfalls. There is a lot of shallow water here too and another reason why it's perhaps one of the best and safest swimming holes to visit. I'd recommend Babinda Boulders if you are travelling with small children. There are plenty of facilities for your trip including toilets, showers, bbq stations, and picnic tables. There's even a free campsite nearby. The other side of Babinda Boulders is the actual boulders, the Devil's Pools. There is a short walk you take and stop at the various viewing platforms to see these incredible views. A lot of this area is fenced off to make it safer for visiting, and signs are there to advise where you can and can't swim. I think in the past, the Devil's Pools were not fenced off and people did swim and climb there, which resulted

71

in casualties and fatalities. As long as you stick to the path, you'll keep safe when visiting. Babinda Boulders are a significant site for the local Aboriginal community, you can learn more about this from the signs when youvisit.

35. JOSEPHINE FALLS

Josephine Falls is another popular swimming spot with locals and tourists. It's just over an hour's drive away from Cairns and a little further south than Babinda Boulders, so it's possible to visit these both in one trip. Josephine Falls is a waterfall with different levels and natural pools to swim in. It's a beautiful sight to see and a great place to spend the day. There is a natural waterslide on the rocks and areas to jump into the water making it perhaps one of the most fun waterfalls to visit. There are plenty of rocks to sit and relax by the water so this makes it a great place for the whole family. The car park is only a short walk away from the water where there are picnic tables and toilet facilities. There are a few different walking tracks from Josephine Falls including to the summit of Mount Bartle Frere.

36. BEHANA GORGE

If you like to walk then this one is for you. To get to the Clamshell Falls at Behana Gorge, there's a long paved walk which is more like a road than a bush walk. It's an easy walk with inclined dips along the way but it's 3.5km long. The path itself is surrounded by trees and the greenery of the rainforest. There are a couple of stunning lookout points along the way and smaller swimming areas. When you reach the falls there are a few different places to swim and little pools to sit in. The Clamshell Falls is a little more dangerous than some of the other swimming holes like Babinda and Josephine. It's a less popular spot so it's calmer and quieter but just as stunning.

37. DAVIES CREEK

Like Windin Falls, Davies Creek has a natural infinity pool but this area is larger to swim in and the walk there is much shorter. There are some incredible lookout points over the falls and several areas to swim. The walk to the main lookout is short but to get into the water you'll need to do a fair bit of scrambling over the rocks. If you like climbing around then you'll love it here. Davies Creek is about an hour away from Cairns, and a less popular spot than some of the others I've mentioned. This makes it one of the more quiet spots where you're likely to bump into more locals. It's another beautiful place to visit if you have the chance.

38. EMERALD CREEK

The final waterfall I'll mention is Emerald Creek. If you want to get into nature and away from the crowds of the city then this one is for you. It's the furthest away from Cairns about an hour and a quarter drive via Mareeba. There is a short 2km walk to get to the main swimming area, where you'll find a rope swing and plenty of space to jump in. You'll need to do a bit of scrambling to get over the rocks but once you're there you can sit back, relax and enjoy the views.

39. MOUNT BARTLE FRERE

Tropical North Queensland is known for its incredible scenery and there are several walks, hikes and viewpoints you can visit to appreciate it. Mount Bartle Frere is the highest mountain in Queensland at 1,611m tall, reaching the summit is a challenge for serious hikers. This steep hike with rock climbing sections starts from Josephine Falls and it's advised that only experienced bushwalkers take on the summit. It's a grade 5 hike, which is the most difficult there is, with a 20km return. It will take around 5 hours to reach the summit from the start point. It can be done in 1 day, but most people allow 2 days so they have plenty of time. The 2 day hike has a stop at Big Rock camp along the way. It's a challenge indeed and some say it's even the most difficult hike in Australia. Those who choose to take on the challenge and succeeded, will be rewarded with the incredible views from the top.

40. WALSH'S PYRAMID

Another summit to reach in Tropical North Queensland is the top of Walsh's Pyramid. This is the tallest natural free-standing pyramid in the world at 922m tall. The walk is much easier than summiting Mount Bartle Frere but it's a challenge nonetheless. The walk is a steep 6km return which on average takes around 6 hours to complete. It's also a grade 5 walking track, which will reward you with incredible views at the top. In August there's the annual Walsh's Pyramid race, where locals compete to race to the summit and back. It takes these runners about an hour and a half to do the entire track with a lot of training in advance. If you're looking for a challenging hike that's not quite as intense as Mount Bartle Frere, then Walsh's Pyramid is a great option for you.

Walsh's Pyramid

41. MAMU TROPICAL SKYWALK

If you fancy a stroll through the rainforest, but want to stay clear of any hiking and intense walking, then visit the Mamu Tropical Skywalk. This is a short boardwalk with an observation deck that looks out into the heart of the Wooroonooran National Park. You can see these amazing views without needing to undertake a difficult and potentially dangerous hike. It's a relaxing walk and the entire experience will take around 2 hours from start to finish. It's perfect for anyone to enjoy. There are plenty of information boards along the way to teach you about the nature you are surrounded by. You do need to buy tickets for this place but you can get some ticket bundles with other activities in the area. I didn't book in advance when I visited on a weekend and it was still relatively quiet. The Skywalk is about an hour and a half drive away from Cairns but a great option to tie into a visit to Babinda Boulders or Josephine Falls. I thoroughly enjoyed this boardwalk and would recommend it to anyone in the area.

42. CAMPBELL'S LOOKOUT

If you want to get a great view of Cairns then visit Campbell's lookout. This viewpoint is just off the side of the road so there is no walking or hiking required. It's perhaps the closest and most accessible lookout in and around Cairns, as it's only a 15 minute drive away from the CBD. You'll get an incredible view of the city and the ocean. This is a great place to stop on your way to visit one of the waterfalls outside of town.

Campbell's Lookout

43. LAKE BARRINE

A different type of day trip if you've seen enough waterfalls and rainforest walks is to visit Lake Barrine. It's a vast lake surrounded by rainforests with a charming little tea cafe. It makes the perfect place to spend a lovely afternoon with friends or family. You can bring a kayak or canoe to paddle around this incredible lake. It's not a common swimming spot although you can swim here. You can also walk the 5km circumference of the lake if you fancy being active.

BEACHES

44. TRINITY BEACH

One of the best beaches to visit whilst staying in Cairns is Trinity Beach. This was one of my favourite spots and it's only a 20 minute drive away. You can also get the bus there if you don't have any transport of your own. It's a beautiful sandy beach, lined with palm trees which provide some much-needed shade. There's usually a net and lifeguard there too if you want to get in the water. On the beachfront, you'll find some shops, restaurants and cafes as well as holiday apartments should you want to stay longer. There's a little walking track nearby so you can get a view of the beach from above. It's a laid-back environment perfect for a relaxing afternoon.

45. PALM COVE

Palm Cove is a popular location about 30 minutes north of Cairns. Here you'll find a relaxed seaside village with shops and restaurants as well as some luxury hotels. A lot of tourists stay in Palm Cove as it's more built up and bigger than the Trinity Beach area, and closer to Port Douglas. The most popular resort is Peppers Beach Club for its impressive facilities and spa-like feel. Palm Cove has a beautiful long sandy beach and plenty of palm trees, there's also a net and lifeguard for swimming. There is a long jetty from the far left side of the beach which is worth walking down as you'll get an incredible view looking back.

46. ELLIS BEACH

Further north to Palm Cove, you'll find Ellis Beach. Similar to Trinity Beach and Palm Cove it's a sand beach surrounded by palm trees with a stinger net for swimming, but it's much smaller and quieter. There's one restaurant nearby and some holiday apartments but otherwise, it feels untouched. You'll feel like you have your own private beach at Ellis Beach.

ADVENTURE SEEKERS

47. BUNGEE JUMP

At 50 metres high, Skypark by AJ Hackett in Cairns is home to the only bungee jump in Australia. If you've never bungee jumped before, then this is the perfect place to tick it off your bucket list. With incredible views from the top and the option to dip into the water below, you're bound to have an exhilarating experience. There are different styles of jumps to suit the more advanced jumpers, and you're free to go and watch from the viewing area below which also serves food and drinks. The Skypark also has a giant swing and a walk-the-plank activity for those who want to feel the rush but aren't quite ready for the big jump. I did my first bungee jump here and would highly recommend it. You can book in advance but they also have available spots on the day if you just turn up. The staff are friendly and make sure you are safe, you even get a free T-shirt included in your ticket price and you can upgrade to have the whole experience videoed.

48. SKYDIVE

What's more adventurous than a bungee jump? How about a skydive? Skydive Australia have many locations all over Australia, one of which is in Cairns. It's the only skydive company in Cairns and you can book your skydive on their website. When the date of your jump arrives, and as long as the weather is looking good, you'll arrive at the store in the CBD. They'll get you prepared and then drive you out to the flight location. You'll fall from 15,000ft with views of the rainforest and the reef below. It's great for first-time jumpers or qualified divers. I did a skydive with Skydive Australia at Mission Beach, one of their other locations about 2 hours drive south of Cairns, and the team was just amazing. They make sure you feel safe, secure and relaxed. I would recommend skydiving over Tropical North Queensland because the views from above are just insane.

49. WHITE WATER RAFTING

If you're looking for something adventurous that doesn't involve jumping or falling from a height then consider white water rafting. This is a popular activity in Tropical North Queensland because of the rivers and rocky terrain. There are a few different tours from Cairns that will usually take you down to Tully River. Guaranteed to provide thrills and entertainment, if you're looking for excitement you're sure to get it white water rafting.

50. FESTIVALS AND EVENTS

Cairns sure knows how to celebrate. They often hold events, celebrations and festivals throughout the year. When I lived there, it always felt like something was going on. There are always signs around the city to tell you what's on and what's coming up. Cairns Festival is an annual event that usually takes place over a week in August and September. There are all sorts of activities and events taking place such as live music, performances and a big parade through the city. Everyone comes from local suburbs to celebrate and have fun together. These events are usually free and you can turn up throughout the event to whatever activities speak to you. Seasonal holidays are also a time for celebration in Cairns. During Christmas time you can of course expect to see a Christmas tree, some exciting light installations and fireworks from the esplanade. They often have different arts and cultural events throughout the year, the calendar is always evolving. Whilst I was there they put on an Italian Festival over the weekend with all sorts of Italian food and music. That's just one example of the fun sort of events and activities that happen all year round in Cairns. During your visit, see what's on and get involved.

BONUS TIPS

BONUS TIP 1. BEST PHOTO SPOTS

Did you really go somewhere if you didn't get the photo to prove it? You'll probably take numerous photos during your visit to Cairns as it's a very photogenic place with some of the most incredible scenery around. However, if you didn't get that perfect shot then here are some of my top recommendations for a great photo.

On the drive to Port Douglas, you'll find Thala Nature Reserve. This is part of the resort but you are allowed to walk around the grounds to take photos, and trust me you will want to. There are rows and rows of beautiful palm trees that make for a stunning backdrop for a photo. If you want to up your photo game pick up the coconuts, use them as props and throw them in the air for a fun shot. If you were looking for a secluded stay in the rainforest then the resort itself is the perfect place. It's an eco-retreat with a private beach!

You don't have to hike up to Walsh's Pyramid to get a great photo. Although a photo from the summit would be incredible, the mountain itself is pretty spectacular and looks great in a photo. On the drive to Behana Gorge, you will drive down a road that looks directly towards Walsh's Pyramid. It's the only way to Behana Gorge and you won't miss it. The road aligns perfectly in the middle making for a stunning shot.

On your visit to Fitzroy Island make sure to get a snap at Nudey Beach, specifically on the swing hanging from the trees. When you arrive at the beach you'll see it on the right-hand side of the trees. Get someone to push you on the swing and take your picture from behind with the beautiful backdrop looking to the ocean.

At the Cairns ZOOM and Wildlife Dome you can take a photo holding a koala. This is an iconic picture that has Australia written all over it.

Taking a selfie with a turtle has to be one of the best pictures you can take in Cairns. If you don't have an underwater camera, don't worry! A lot of people get waterproof pouches for their phones to take some epic shots under the water. If you want to get some amazing shots of The Great Barrier Reef and the marine wildlife that lives there, consider renting a Go-Pro for the day. The Calypso shop near the reef fleet terminal rents Go-Pros. Pop by in advance to let them know you want to book one out and then you can collect it on the morning before youe trip. It's a great way to capture some amazing memories without needing to buy any equipment outright.

As Cairns is on the east coast, there aren't many sunset spots. However, I stumbled upon a little hidden gem which is the perfect place to watch the sunset and get some beautiful snaps. You'll want to head to Yorkeys Knob about a 20 minute drive north of Cairns. There is a main beach here but that's not the one you want. Look on the map and head to the tiny little patch of sand next to the Boating Club on Buckley Street. This is a modest beach but it's slightly north facing so you can appreciate the sun setting and get a pretty picture.

BONUS TIP 2. DATE SPOT TO IMPRESS

If you're celebrating a special occasion and are looking for somewhere to go head to Rocco by Crystalbrook. It's a tall glass building on the esplanade, you can't miss it. This might be the most impressive date night spot in all of Cairns. This luxury rooftop restaurant is on the 12th floor of the hotel providing some incredible views from the top. Enjoy sipping on the signature cocktails while you gaze out into the ocean. Be sure to book in advance and prepare to impress.

BONUS TIP 3. SERIOUS WALKING

I've given you some of the best hikes in Tropical North Queensland, but I'll leave you with one more. This is for you serious hikers out there who just can't get enough. It's not as intense as Mount Bartle Frere or Walsh's Pyramid, at a grade 4 walk. To start, head towards Barron Gorge and park in the Stoney Creek car park. It's a 7km round trip and a gentle ascent to the top. It's a long walk, not the most difficult in the area but you should still have a good level of fitness before attempting to tackle it. The views from the top are as amazing as you can imagine, you'll feel like you're in the clouds. On the return, take a dip in Stoney Creek to have a much-needed cooldown.

BONUS TIP 4. DRESS LIKE THE LOCALS

There are lots of places to buy clothes in Cairns, but if you want to experience some of the local independent stores visit Oceana Walk Shopping Arcade. This is in the heart of the CBD and is home to some fun shops and little cafes. Explore the rails in Vintage Seeker, buy a dress at Gypsett, and get your nails done. Then grab a coffee at Blackbird Laneway espresso bar or an energising tea from Tropik Nutrition and finish off with a bite to eat at Pantry 15 or Candy Lane. You'll be sure to bump heads with locals in this area of town.

BONUS TIP 5. USEFUL APPS

Today we're in the digital age and your smartphone is more than likely taking the trip to Cairns with you. Here are some apps which you should download before you arrive in Cairns to make your visit that much smoother.

Booking, Hostel World & Agoda are great apps to book any accommodation you might need during your trip.

XE Currency App allows you to compare different currencies quickly and easily. It can be especially useful when you arrive in Australia if you are not familiar with the AUD exchange rate.

Beam is the app you'll need to hire electric scooters and bikes during your trip to Cairns. You'll need to add your credit card, but it won't deduct any money until you take your first ride.

WikiCamps is a paid app but once you've paid for the app you get it for a lifetime as there are no subscriptions. This app is ideal for anyone who is planning on camping or travelling around and camping across Australia. It shows you all the different camp spots and facilities. You can even download it and use it offline when you're in more remote parts of the country.

Cairns Taxis has its own app which can be great if you plan to take a few taxis whilst in the city.

BONUS TIP 6. MUDDY'S PLAYGROUND

A great spot in Cairns for parents and families is Muddy's Playground. Located on the esplanade, this playground is a fun way to keep children of all ages entertained. There are various areas to play in and some water features. They also have a good cafe that serves up incredible food and drinks that everyone can enjoy. The added view of the ocean is a bonus.

BONUS TIP 7. CAPE TRIBULATION

If you have more time to spend around the area of North Queensland then I would highly recommend a trip to Cape Tribulation. You can do this in a day trip but it is over a 2.5 hour drive away from Cairns. There's plenty to do you'll want to stay at least one night, maybe more. I fell in love with Cape Tribulation and being immersed in the Daintree Rainforest. The beaches here are beautiful and the perfect place to watch the sunrise. Do not swim in the ocean here as crocodiles do inhabit the area. You'll be perfectly safe sitting on the sand where the Daintree Rainforest meets The Great Barrier Reef. It's an incredible and impressive place to be. If you are staying overnight, I would recommend PK's Jungle Village. This is one of the most popular budget accommodations, there is a lively bar and restaurant that many locals visit. It's right by Myall Beach and will take just a 5 minute walk in the morning to catch the sunrise. Cape Trib Beach House is another popular accommodation, and there are many other luxury cabin-style hotels in the area.

Around Cape Tribulation, there are plenty of boardwalks to get immersed in the Daintree Rainforest, which is the oldest rainforest in the world! Kulki Boardwalk is a very short walk to a nice lookout, Dubuji Boardwalk is a longer walk that takes you out to Myall Beach, and Marrdja Boardwalk takes you around the mangroves. However, the boardwalk I enjoyed the most was the Jindalba Boardwalk as it had some of the most incredible scenery. Keep your eyes peeled for Southern Cassowaries along these walks as they roam the area. You can also visit the Daintree Discovery Centre if you want to explore more and learn about the area.

Whilst in Cape Tribulation, pay a visit to the Daintree Ice Cream Company. They make all different flavours of ice cream with fruit grown on the farm. Try the signature cup for a mix of flavours they have that day. It will be a combination of your typical favourites and some exotic fruits you probably haven't heard of before. You can enjoy your ice cream whilst you walk around the farm and see the fruits growing.

I'd recommend hiring a car yourself and taking the trip to Cape Tribulation, but you can go on an organised tour setting off from Cairns.

BONUS TIP 8. CAPE TRIBULATION SWIMMING HOLES

Even though you can't swim in the sea in Cape Tribulation, there are a few swimming holes you can visit.

Mason's swimming hole is a small one in the middle of Cape Tribulation. Although it might be small compared to some of the waterfalls around Cairns, there is plenty of room for a little swim. It's pretty amazing to be swimming surrounded by the rainforest as this area is mostly enclosed by trees. It's a popular spot so it can be quite busy, there's also a cafe on the way to the watering hole.

Emmagen Creek is another swimming hole further north. This one is much less busy as it's further out. You can get here with a 2WD but just go easy. There's a little walk to get to the water but then you have plenty of space to swim.

Perhaps the best swimming hole in the area is Mossman Gorge. This one is en route from Cairns to

Cape Tribulation. You park at the visitor centre and then buy a shuttle ticket to reach the gorge itself. Do not walk or drive to the gorge as this is home to an aboriginal community and the purpose of the shuttle is to minimise disturbance in the area. The shuttles run frequently and it's only a short journey away. It's a popular spot to visit but there's plenty of room for everyone to swim. The gorge is surrounded by trees and it feels like a fairytale. You can also walk along the path beside the gorge to get to an incredible viewpoint.

BONUS TIP 9. COW BAY BEACH

On your drive to Cape Tribulation, you should stop at Cow Bay beach. This beach is beautiful with its white sand, blue sea and palm trees. It's quiet and feels secluded. You can't swim here because of crocs but it's a lovely place for a little walk. Also, look out for the rope swing for some fun and nice photos.

BONUS TIP 10. MOUNT ALEXANDRA LOOKOUT

The final tip when visiting the Cape Tribulation area is to stop at the Mount Alexandra Lookout. You can drive right up to it and stop to take a look. The view looks outwards onto the sea between the trees, it's breathtaking. The point at which you're looking out is also the beach where Steve Irwin got injured by the Stingray. Although that's not the nicest image, let it be a reminder of his legacy and the incredible nature and wildlife right before your eyes.

Myall Beach

TOP REASONS TO BOOK THIS TRIP

The Great Barrier Reef: One of the seven wonders of the natural world, once you visit The Great Barrier Reef from Cairns you will understand why it is so special.

Waterfalls: Cairns is surrounded by an abundance of incredible waterfalls, take a dip in these cold waters and feel a rush of energy and excitement.

Tropical Terrain: From the tropical beaches to the rainforest you'll find amazing wildlife, beautiful plants and varying incredible landscapes.

PACKING AND PLANNING TIPS

A Week before Leaving

- Arrange for someone to take care of pets and water plants.

- Email and Print important Documents.

- Get Visa and vaccines if needed.

- Check for travel warnings.

- Stop mail and newspaper.

- Notify Credit Card companies where you are going.

- Passports and photo identification is up to date.

- Pay bills.

- Copy important items and download travel Apps.

- Start collecting small bills for tips.

- Have post office hold mail while you are away.

- Check weather for the week.

- Car inspected, oil is changed, and tires have the correct pressure.

- Check airline luggage restrictions.

- Download Apps needed for your trip.

Right Before Leaving

- Contact bank and credit cards to tell them your location.

- Clean out refrigerator.

- Empty garbage cans.

- Lock windows.

- Make sure you have the proper identification with you.

- Bring cash for tips.

- Remember travel documents.

- Lock door behind you.

- Remember wallet.

- Unplug items in house and pack chargers.

- Change your thermostat settings.

- Charge electronics, and prepare camera memory cards.

READ OTHER GREATER THAN A TOURIST BOOKS

> TOURIST

Follow us on Instagram for beautiful travel images:
http://Instagram.com/GreaterThanATourist

Follow *Greater Than a Tourist* on Amazon.

CZYKPublishing.com

Resources

Cairns Taxis - Download the app or call (07) 4048 8333 to book a taxi.
Backpacker Deals is a great website to book tours in Cairns and all over Australia - https://www.backpackerdeals.com/australia/cairns

Justin Bainbridge Youtube Channel - https://www.youtube.com/@JustinBainbridgeYT
I lived in Cairns and explored with Justin and he has made many videos about the area. I highly recommend you watch them if you'd like some more information and visuals.
Cairns Travel Guide - https://www.youtube.com/watch?v=G9-BpIpawhM
Cairns City Travel Guide - https://www.youtube.com/watch?v=2H0r9bNyqDY
Port Douglas Travel Guide - https://www.youtube.com/watch?v=QfXr7uuhXG0&t=2s
Fitzroy Island Travel Guide - https://www.youtube.com/watch?v=hWp3Tak24Tk
The Great Barrier Reef - https://www.youtube.com/watch?v=QnQPSYC3Idl
Cape Tribulation - https://www.youtube.com/watch?v=oAcEC99WqA8
Skydive Australia - https://www.youtube.com/watch?v=NYvAAABUIVE

Bungee Jump - https://www.youtube.com/watch?v=wfjPMddQGys

Kuranda Rainforest Skyrail - https://www.youtube.com/watch?v=2oIJyA4YLkk

Top 10 Waterfalls In Queensland - https://www.youtube.com/watch?v=Nj3Tsz_ZeBQ

Milla Milla & Nandroya Falls - https://www.youtube.com/watch?v=sH4mrOcgAqs

Windin Falls - https://www.youtube.com/watch?v=wD2oO6GtPLk

Crystal Cascades - https://www.youtube.com/watch?v=4EBp9v0EGGc

Emerald Creek Falls - https://www.youtube.com/watch?v=E2d4SWFq0Ps

Davies Creek Falls - https://www.youtube.com/watch?v=Sf1kXj4dxdc&t=1s

Glacier Rock - https://www.youtube.com/watch?v=Pf_v-8C5MjM

> TOURIST

At *Greater Than a Tourist*, we love to share travel tips with you. How did we do? What guidance do you have for how we can give you better advice for your next trip? Please send your feedback to CZYKPublishing@gmail.com as we continue to improve the series. We appreciate your constructive feedback. Thank you.

METRIC CONVERSIONS

TEMPERATURE

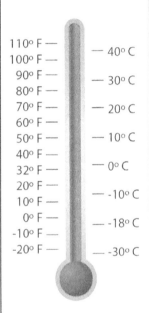

110° F —	— 40° C
100° F —	
90° F —	— 30° C
80° F —	
70° F —	— 20° C
60° F —	
50° F —	— 10° C
40° F —	
32° F —	— 0° C
20° F —	
10° F —	— -10° C
0° F —	
-10° F —	— -18° C
-20° F —	— -30° C

To convert F to C:

Subtract 32, and then multiply by 5/9 or .5555.

To Convert C to F:

Multiply by 1.8 and then add 32.

32F = 0C

LIQUID VOLUME

To Convert:...............Multiply by
U.S. Gallons to Liters................ 3.8
U.S. Liters to Gallons 26
Imperial Gallons to U.S. Gallons 1.2
Imperial Gallons to Liters....... 4.55
Liters to Imperial Gallons 22
1 Liter = .26 U.S. Gallon
1 U.S. Gallon = 3.8 Liters

DISTANCE

To convert ....Multiply by
Inches to Centimeters 2.54
Centimeters to Inches 39
Feet to Meters...................... .3
Meters to Feet 3.28
Yards to Meters 91
Meters to Yards 1.09
Miles to Kilometers 1.61
Kilometers to Miles............ .62
1 Mile = 1.6 km
1 km = .62 Miles

WEIGHT

1 Ounce = .28 Grams
1 Pound = .4555 Kilograms
1 Gram = .04 Ounce
1 Kilogram = 2.2 Pounds

TRAVEL QUESTIONS

- Do you bring presents home to family or friends after a vacation?

- Do you get motion sick?

- Do you have a favorite billboard?

- Do you know what to do if there is a flat tire?

- Do you like a sun roof open?

- Do you like to eat in the car?

- Do you like to wear sun glasses in the car?

- Do you like toppings on your ice cream?

- Do you use public bathrooms?

- Did you bring a cell phone and does it have power?

- Do you have a form of identification with you?

- Have you ever been pulled over by a cop?

- Have you ever given money to a stranger on a road trip?

- Have you ever taken a road trip with animals?

- Have you ever gone on a vacation alone?

- Have you ever run out of gas?

- If you could move to any place in the world, where would it be?

- If you could travel anywhere in the world, where would you travel?

- If you could travel in any vehicle, which one would it be?

- If you had three things to wish for from a magic genie, what would they be?

- If you have a driver's license, how many times did it take you to pass the test?

- What are you the most afraid of on vacation?

- What do you want to get away from the most when you are on vacation?

- What foods smell bad to you?

- What item do you bring on ever trip with you away from home?

- What makes you sleepy?

- What song would you love to hear on the radio when you're cruising on the highway?

- What travel job would you want the least?

- What will you miss most while you are away from home?

- What is something you always wanted to try?

- What is the best road side attraction that you ever saw?

- What is the farthest distance you ever biked?

- What is the farthest distance you ever walked?

- What is the weirdest thing you needed to buy while on vacation?

- What is your favorite candy?

- What is your favorite color car?

- What is your favorite family vacation?

- What is your favorite food?

- What is your favorite gas station drink or food?

- What is your favorite license plate design?

- What is your favorite restaurant?

- What is your favorite smell?

- What is your favorite song?

- What is your favorite sound that nature makes?

- What is your favorite thing to bring home from a vacation?

- What is your favorite vacation with friends?

- What is your favorite way to relax?

- Where is the farthest place you ever traveled in a car?

- Where is the farthest place you ever went North, South, East and West?

- Where is your favorite place in the world?

- Who is your favorite singer?

- Who taught you how to drive?

- Who will you miss the most while you are away?

- Who if the first person you will contact when you get to your destination?

- Who brought you on your first vacation?

- Who likes to travel the most in your life?

- Would you rather be hot or cold?

- Would you rather drive above, below, or at the speed limited?

- Would you rather drive on a highway or a back road?

- Would you rather go on a train or a boat?

- Would you rather go to the beach or the woods?

>TOURIST

Made in the USA
Las Vegas, NV
12 February 2025

18007050R00075